THE THREAT SWITCH

The Secret to Creating Breakthrough High-Performance Teams

RANDY YOST

INDIE BOOKS
INTERNATIONAL

ISBN-10: 1-947480-34-0
ISBN-13: 978-1-947480-34-6
Library of Congress Control Number: 2018959511

The Threat Switch™ is a pending trademark of Randy Yost
Breakthrough High-Performance Teams™ is a pending trademark of Randy Yost
Whac-A-Mole is a trademark of Mattel, Inc.

Designed by Joni McPherson, mcphersongraphics.com

INDIE BOOKS INTERNATIONAL, LLC
2424 VISTA WAY, SUITE 316
OCEANSIDE, CA 92054
www.indiebooksintl.com

THE THREAT SWITCH

CONTENTS

PART I

WHY BETTER THINKING CREATES BREAKTHROUGH

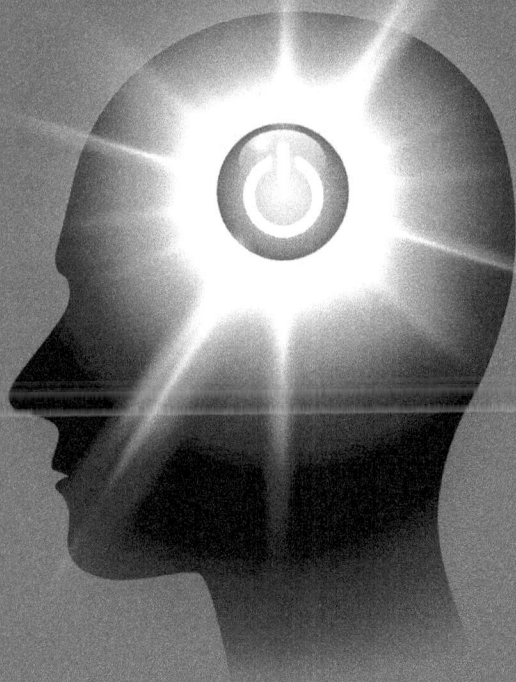

Chapter 1

The Threat Switch: Enemy Number One of Breakthrough Teams

Fred Penman was a problem-solver. When builders and public agencies in Sacramento had a problem with tough terrain and obstacles, they turned to Fred, the construction operations manager at Western Engineering Contractors in Loomis, California.

One day as Fred tried to decipher a stack of handwritten field records, he knew he had a problem. How could he get all of his field foremen to upgrade record-keeping from pen and paper to portable, handheld computers?

Fred decided to pursue the goal: a handheld computer in the hands of every foreman within a year's time. He set up a meeting to explain the logic of switching to the digital age.

But soon, there was conflict. When Fred approached the field foremen with the idea, he got a lot of pushback. Fred explained, encouraged, and even harangued the foremen about the benefits of switching to the handheld electronic devices, all to no avail.

The foremen fought Fred on the issue, complaining bitterly about the difficulty of changing their record-keeping from paper to electronic records, despite the benefits. Tempers flared during the meeting.

"C'mon Fred, give us a break. We are up to our eyeballs in mass grading and utility installation projects," said a veteran foreman named Ben. "And now we should drop everything and learn some computer program? A pen and paper form work just fine, and are a lot cheaper too."

Now, Fred's natural inclination usually would have been to fight with the foremen over the issue. After all, he was the boss and what the boss says goes. But instead of fight, he chose flight.

"Fine, just fine," said Fred, as he stood up and walked out of the conference room.

That's when Fred sought me out, and we discussed the Breakthrough, High-Performance Team approach to managing the change.

"Fred, they flipped The Threat Switch in your brain," I advised him. "It was fight, freeze, or flight. You choose flight, and that is only natural. Even if they flip The Threat Switch on, remember you have the power to flip it back off."

Fred brought the foremen back to the table. Instead of fighting them with top-down leadership, Fred encouraged the foremen to engage in making the change work for them.

"You are well-seasoned and experienced engineers," Fred calmly told the team, "so you engineer how we upgrade."

Once the foremen could participate in figuring out the best way to use the new equipment and were allowed to make decisions regarding the implementation, they took ownership of the project.

Within three months, when Fred toured the projects, he saw every foreman was using a handheld device for field reports. Back at the office, Fred could easily read the field reports that crossed his desk.

After a couple of months of going digital, one foreman approached Fred and said, "I am glad we thought of this. All of the foremen agree we would never go back to pen and paper again."

Living with The Threat Switch

"When we do what comes naturally, we stand to lose." A wise mentor named Bern Moses (really, his name was Moses) told me that a long time ago. It took me years to really understand what he meant.

Moses was telling me that a part of our brain is designed for one thing: survival. This brain part often dictates our behavior, consciously and subconsciously. In anatomy and neuroscience, it is called the amygdala, and it is often referred to as our lizard (reptilian) brain. This part of the brain helps us survive by dictating whether we choose to fight, flee, or freeze.

I call the lizard brain The Threat Switch. This ancient part of our brain is only the size of an almond (amygdala is Greek for almond), but it has huge power.

When the amygdala detects a possible threat to our survival, it immediately hijacks the brain and engages our fight, flee, or freeze reaction mechanism. This is quite a natural action.

The challenge all people face is that the amygdala doesn't differentiate between a *real* life-or-death threat situation or a *perceived* life-or-death threat situation. The Threat Switch reacts the same whether someone is coming at you with a baseball bat or telling you that they think your idea is stupid. The amygdala has only two positions—on or off—and once it senses a threat, it goes into action.

Moses explained that humans do not have to allow their amygdala to dictate their behavior when the situation is not life-threatening. Simply tell The Threat Switch you're not going to die, so back off. Hence, you do not have to do what comes naturally. You can be *supra*natural. Being supranatural means knowingly and purposefully not doing what comes naturally.

So, what does it mean to be supranatural, in practical terms? The best way I have found to take back control from the amygdala is to focus on asking clarification questions. This act of being intentionally supranatural redirects blood flow from the amygdala to the cerebral cortex, where human genius and creativity reside, not where our survival lizard resides.

Mechanism

Ah, the amygdala. Clinical studies including brain scans and neurocircuitry mapping have allowed scientists to understand more about how the brain is structured and how it works. It has become well recognized and accepted that emotional intelligence resides in a part of the brain called the limbic system. Proof of this is best evidenced from several medical cases in which a person's limbic system has been damaged, and the person has lost the ability to experience emotions or feelings.

Within the limbic system resides the amygdala and its fight, flight, or freeze response. Virtually all animals have this survival instinct hard-wired into their brains. While this mechanism is crucial to our survival, it often takes over at work when it is not needed, resulting in inappropriate and often damaging behavior to ourselves and others on the team.

How often have you experienced or seen another person engage in the fight, freeze, or flight response during the course of a business meeting?

A typical example: one team member shares a solution regarding an issue at hand, and a second team member quickly states that the proposed solution is wrong and gives his or her own solution. What happens? Most likely a disagreement ensues in which each person defends his or her solution (fight), or one of the team members will capitulate to the other, not agreeing but not willing to argue (freeze). I have seen team members actually push themselves away from the table or leave the room (flight).

Here is a typical business scenario to illustrate. A customer is demanding a cash refund for not getting a product on time. The team discussion might go something like this:

Team member one: "I think we should refund 10 percent of the price to maintain a positive relationship with this customer." (*Neutral.*)

Team member two: "Wrong! This customer is always complaining. A refund would just encourage them to complain more." (*Fight.*)

Team member one: "That's just stupid. This customer is a big account. No way we should antagonize them more." (*Fight.*)

Team member two: "You're calling me stupid? What's stupid is being wimps in front of these guys." (*Fight.*)

Team member one: "Fine, whatever. Are we done here?" (*Flight.*)

Interestingly, the amygdala's natural response to even a perceived threat like the episode above is to hijack the brain and force the fight, freeze, or flight response to drive behavior. Rational thought leaves the room, and chaos often ensues.

The key to dealing with the amygdala's natural reaction to a perceived threat is to take command of one's thoughts and instruct the amygdala that survival is not at stake, so lighten up. This takes some training and practice, but the rewards for both the individual and the organization can be spectacular. When team members do not allow the amygdalae (that's plural) in the room to take over, they are able to work together to find the best solution to an issue and not waste time or energy arguing about and defending who is right or wrong.

In short, team members engage in an emotionally intelligent discussion. This is so important because when The Threat Switch takes control, trust is absent. Research conducted at the Deming Center for Quality Management found 50 percent of time wasted in business is due to lack of trust.

A lack of trust seems to be natural in business. The secret to creating Breakthrough, High-Performance Teams is to *not do what comes naturally*. That is explored in the following chapter.

AXIOMS FOR HIGH PERFORMANCE

The Threat Switch: Enemy Number One of Breakthrough, High-Performance Teams

- Do not allow The Threat Switch to drive your thoughts or actions.

- If someone flips your Threat Switch, flip it off and seek first to understand.

- You do not have to choose fight, flight, or freeze; there are other options.

- You do not have to do what comes naturally; you can be supranatural.

Chapter 2

Put Aside What Comes Naturally

I have spent the majority of my life deliberately studying human behavior, taking the praxeology approach, which is the deliberate study of human behavior from a streetwise, practical approach.

This practical approach is the converse of theory. While I obtained a bachelor of arts degree in business administration and a minor in psychology, 95 percent of my business and human behavior acumen comes from personal challenges and leadership experience.

You can accomplish a great deal with breakthrough, high-performance teams if you put aside what comes naturally. The story of my journey illustrates this point.

The Threat Switch and Me

Two seminal events in my life have determined and guided my ongoing curiosity and research regarding human behavior.

As a young man, I had elective surgery to lengthen my hamstrings to correct a birth defect. As the saying goes, the operation was a success, but the patient (almost) died. Shortly after the operation, I was informed I would most likely never be able to walk again. As you can imagine, this news was devastating. I seriously considered doing away with myself.

Fortunately, there were people in my life who eventually convinced me to get on with life. I did, but for a very long time, horrible behavior was my way of being. For more than five years, I viewed the world as a cruel, unfair place. I struggled constantly with depression, hateful thoughts, and actions. This made me and those around me miserable.

When presenting at a workshop, I often ask if people feel I was justified in my beliefs and behavior regarding the results of the operation. Almost always the answer is a resounding "yes." When I ask if they think that the behavior was beneficial to me, all respond with a rousing "no." Of course, they are right.

So, the question becomes, why did I insist on engaging in bad behavior when it only made things worse? I eventually figured out that my behavior was driven by fear (enter the amygdala, a.k.a., The Threat Switch).

By learning to control my fear, I was able to get in command of my behavior and even learn to walk (in a fashion) again. While the entire episode was a horrific personal experience, it did spark my lifelong interest in an age-old human question.

Why do we often behave in a manner that is hurtful and detrimental to ourselves and others?

The second life experience that provided an opportunity for studying human behavior in a difficult environment was my career as a bank turnaround CEO. By accident of being at the right (or wrong) place at the right (or wrong) time, I became the CEO of a failing bank in the mid-1980s. That began a fifteen-year period of working at several banks in danger of violating regulatory orders, which could have resulted in the banks being forcibly closed.

As you can imagine, the atmosphere at these banks was one of fear. The employees feared losing their jobs, the board members feared their personal and group liability, the shareholders feared losing their investment, and the customers feared losing their bank. As bad as it was, the financial condition of these banks was not the most difficult challenge; it was the attitude and behavior of the individuals who feared the consequences of bank failure.

Employees, board members, shareholders, and customers all engaged in significant fear-based behaviors: fighting (with each other), fleeing (mentally checking out), and freezing (deer in the headlights). Did this behavior promote getting the banks turned around and back on their financial footing? Absolutely not, and yet as mentioned previously, my biggest challenge was getting folks to behave, both as individuals and a team, in a way that would support rebuilding the financial foundation of the bank, not focusing on who was to blame for the past. Fortunately, we succeeded in most situations. This leadership experience greatly expanded my learning and understanding about human performance and how to positively affect my behavior and the behavior of others.

Since my banking experience, for the past twenty years, my career has included coaching hundreds of CEOs, presidents, and business leaders. During this time, the only consistent differentiator and competitive advantage identified by companies in our ever-changing and dynamic business environment is people.

An obvious question becomes, what causes people to behave in *beneficial* ways?

The answer is that they have a high level of emotional intelligence. This type of intelligence gives them the ability to foster a state of mind that allows them to think, behave, and act in a positive and optimistic manner, regardless of what's happening in their environment. "Stuff" still happens; emotionally intelligent people just deal with it differently. They are self-aware and self-managed. They are able to motivate themselves and others, have genuine empathy, and are socially influential.

Why Banking Wasn't Boring

When I first started in banking in the early 1970s, it was a very static environment. Banking hadn't changed much since the Great Depression of the 1930s.

I remember one of my college business professors telling me that I would quickly become bored in banking. Banks took in deposits at 3 percent and made loans at 6 percent, end of story.

That professor was so wrong. Banking was about to enter an extremely dynamic period which I found interesting and challenging. New regulations, new types of products, and new customer expectations all led to a far more complicated and risky business environment.

As a result, in the 1980s the number of bank failures skyrocketed across the nation. The environment had quickly become far too dynamic and risky, with a multitude of strategic and tactical issues creating roadblocks and bottlenecks. This new, more dynamic environment was affecting virtually all types of industries.

In my experience as a bank CEO, one thing became very clear, very fast: running a business is a lot like playing the game Whac-a-Mole. If you have never seen one, Whac-A-Mole is a popular arcade game invented in the 1970s. The machine has five holes, and once the game starts, moles pop up from the holes at random. The object of the game is to use a rubber mallet to quickly hit the moles and force them back into their holes.

This was banking in the 1980s.

When a problem popped up, you attacked it. It seemed as soon as one crisis was dealt with, another popped up, over and over again. The executive team, including myself, spent most of our time whacking at threats, not making much forward progress. We needed a way to get rid of the moles (problems) *before* they popped up.

Out of necessity, we invented the concept of breakthrough, high-performance teams to get rid of the moles once and for all. Our definition was: "Breakthrough, high-performance teams attack challenges and embrace opportunities on an ongoing basis, achieving goals and getting desired results."

After banking, I went into executive coaching and have run leadership groups for the past twenty years as a chair for Vistage International, a worldwide community of more than 21,000 CEOs, business owners, and key executives committed to making great decisions that benefit their companies, families, and communities.

Founded in 1957, Vistage places business leaders in confidential peer advisory boards who meet monthly to tackle their toughest business and leadership challenges and maximize opportunities. A chair facilitates the meetings and provides one-to-one coaching. Members build on their monthly meetings with an extensive platform that includes expert speakers, original research and thought leadership, networking events, and a global online community.

Sad to say, in the hundreds of companies I have worked with, I have found that business Whac-a-Mole is a common sport. Breakthrough, high-performance teams are the way to deal with internal bottleneck and roadblock threats and keep them from popping up in the first place.

Quest Diagnostics

I was fortunate to be an executive coach to Tim Burke, president of Quest Diagnostics, for over twenty years.

When I first met Tim in 1997, he shocked me and his fellow Vistage members by telling us that in the IT world, he needed to dramatically change his company's business model every eighteen months. Today, he says it's every six months.

Companies must have an ongoing, internal mechanism which allows them to identify and adjust to a constantly changing business environment. The old, top-down leadership approach is simply inadequate in our increasingly dynamic environment, as it does not apply sufficient brainpower to identify and solve the multitude of roadblocks and bottlenecks constantly surfacing in today's dynamic businesses. The Breakthrough, High-Performance Team approach dramatically increases a company's team brainpower, enabling organizations to thrive in our dynamic business environment.

The Origin of Breakthrough, High-Performance Teams

"This is a federal cease-and-desist order," said the bank examiner. "You have eighteen months to get this bank's loan portfolio and profitability into compliance, or we are shutting you down."

Back in the 1980s, my bank had many turnaround challenges to tackle. And the clock was ticking. As CEO, I knew a top-down approach was not going to fix the bank's woes in time. I needed more brainpower, and I needed it fast.

I assembled my fourteen branch managers and put the problem to them.

"You are now the branch management team, and your job as a team is to identify issues that need attention, figure out the roadblocks that are in our way, and find the bottlenecks," I told the team.

At first, there was some pushback.

"I am not sure we can fix this in time," one manager said. "This is going to take a breakthrough."

What happened next was like the scene in the film *Apollo 13*, when a group of rocket scientists were assembled to figure out how to bring the three astronauts in the damaged spaceship home. Those rocket scientists were told that failure was not an option; the branch managers knew failure was not an option for them, either.

"If we don't figure this out," said one branch manager, "this means closures and the death of the bank."

No branch manager was interested in that option.

But fixing the bank was not easy. The first aspect the branch management team attacked was making the invisible visible. They quickly identified the elephants in the room—the issues that the managers had not wanted to openly discuss before. In truth, it takes a great deal of brainpower to ignore the elephants in the room, to keep the invisible issues invisible. This keeps The Threat Switch in command, because the brain is driven by fear.

Once the issues were all identified and out in the open (and no one died), it sparked a surge of creativity. Since brains no longer had to focus on fear, the team's brains were now free to focus on solutions.

When it came to challenges, the motto became: "Name it, nail it, get rid of it." Internal roadblocks were cleared out of the way. Nobody accepted excuses like, "we've always done it this way," or, "we don't have enough resources."

What happened next is what I came to term the "behavioral cascade." In my experience, I have found that jointly held beliefs determine team culture. In turn, culture drives behavior. And finally, behavior drives results.

Some beliefs are limiting. In business, these are beliefs like "The market is stagnant" or "We can't recruit enough good salespeople." When The Threat Switch is in control, fear creates beliefs that justify a lack of results.

Here is the classic example of a limiting belief. Before 1954, the world's great runners thought a sub-four-minute mile was impossible. When Roger Bannister of England ran a sub-four-minute mile, then world-class runners finally believed it was possible. A culture was created. Many runners subsequently ran the mile in under four minutes. Today, that culture has spread so far and wide that even high-school runners run sub-four-minute miles. Beliefs drove culture, then culture drove behavior, and behavior drove results.

The opposite of a limiting belief is an empowering belief. Here are examples of empowering beliefs:

> *We have a strong, growing market with many potential customers.*

> *We can have a strong marketing program over the next eighteen months.*

We have high-quality people who can exceed market opportunities.

When I wanted to be a Vistage chair in Reno, Nevada in 1997, I ran into a limiting belief. The senior management of Vistage thought Reno was not a big enough town to support a Vistage group because there were not that many CEOs in the region. My empowering belief was, "Reno is a growing market with many potential Vistage members." I talked the senior executives at Vistage into letting me try.

With the traditional Vistage recruitment approach, it was difficult to find members. But then I tapped into the power of a smaller community connection. Many of the CEOs in the area were connected through membership in Rotary, an international service organization. So, I joined Rotary and soon was invited to give a presentation on what I do. This led me to forming *three* Vistage groups in Reno, with 70 percent of the members coming out of Rotary.

To their pleasant surprise, my success changed the thinking of Vistage leadership about the size of the town. Like the milers after Bannister, Vistage now believed it was possible to form groups in towns even smaller than Reno. This shift led to substantial growth for the organization in small markets.

My practical research into limiting beliefs and empowering beliefs has led to five key ways to create breakthrough, high-performance teams. These critical five elements are examined in detail in part II of this book.

Axioms for High Performance

Put Aside What Comes Naturally

- No business wins the game of Whac-a-Mole; you win by eliminating the game.

- Embrace change and consider it a challenge and opportunity.

- Be receptive to others' ideas.

- Contribute actively and purposefully to make things better.

- Live life as a celebration, enjoying what life has to offer.

PART II

FIVE STEPS TO CREATE BREAKTHROUGH, HIGH-PERFORMANCE TEAMS

Chapter 3

Build Trust

L ouie always thought of himself as a straight shooter. As the general service manager for a Caterpillar dealer in Northern California, it was important to Louie that he was known as trustworthy. He was a man of few words who did not like to waste time.

The day Louie read the results of the team's assessment of him, he was shocked. This was a crisis moment for Louie, and he knew he needed to do something about it. For the question, whether he was "open, straightforward, and above-board, with no hidden agenda," Louie rated himself 10 on a 10-point scale. His fellow managers collectively rated him 6.4. "Ouch; I do not deserve this," thought Louie.

I was brought in to help the company pursue creating a breakthrough, high-performance team. The disclosure from colleagues that Louie had a hidden agenda was the elephant in the room that needed to be discussed. To help Louie build trust, a frank discussion was needed.

Steps needed to be taken to get to the bottom of the trust issue; this process can produce conflict. A lively discussion ensued regarding why Louie had been rated so low by his peers. David, one of the first to speak, pointed out that he had requested pay raises for some of his employees many times, and each time he received the same terse response from Louie: "No." Other team managers began to pile on, criticizing Louie for the same curt responses to their requests.

Louie did not like conflict, but finally opened up to the group about a recent meeting with his team. "So, we are having this meeting, and I tell my managers my bonus last quarter was only $258 bucks. I don't know if you guys think I am on some pedestal, but I am not making huge amounts of money. I told them, 'If you aren't getting bonuses, I am not getting bonuses.'"

The mood changed in the meeting once Louie finally opened up. They found out Louie wasn't hoarding money to enrich himself, which was what they had thought was his hidden agenda.

"It changed the atmosphere, because I exposed myself and became vulnerable," said Louie. "I laid it all on the table, including my salary. Now, they saw that I was being genuine, and it suddenly felt more comfortable in the room."

Louie's trustworthiness took a giant leap forward from then on.

Trust Is the Foundation

In the beginning, there must be trust. In fact, trust is foundational for creating a breakthrough, high-performance team. If a high level of trust cannot be created, then the team will never progress to a breakthrough, high-performance team.

Genuine vulnerability, that state of mind that allows for curiosity and learning, is crucial to developing trust. Interestingly, most people perceive vulnerability in themselves as a weakness. Ironically, these same people perceive another person's willingness to be vulnerable as a strength.

I have seen this phenomenon many times in Vistage meetings, where CEOs are hesitant to be vulnerable for fear of losing respect in the group. Yet these same CEOs verbalize respect and admiration when fellow members engage in vulnerability.

Ground Rules for Trust

Certain ground rules have to be agreed upon to allow team members the safety to be vulnerable in meetings when you are creating breakthrough, high-performance teams. Here are a few:

- **Make the invisible visible.** Don't allow an elephant in the room. Have the courage to talk about the real issue.

- **Truly listen.** Work to listen and not interrupt when others' ideas and opinions are expressed. Listening does not mean waiting until the other person is finished speaking.

- **Seek first to understand.** Try to see issues from the other person's viewpoint.

- **Ask clarification questions.** Words and phrases mean different things to different people. Jargon can also get in the way of communications.

- **Repeat to verify.** Repeat what you heard, so other people know they have been understood.

- **Avoid fear-causing words or statements.** These include: "You are wrong," "I disagree," and, "That's a dumb idea."

One Bad Apple

I will never forget the day I met Fred, the hard-working founder of a staffing firm. Fred had grown the firm from zero to thirty-plus people through the years, but now faced a crossroads.

As I started to work with the five members of Fred's leadership team, the main challenge soon became obvious. His senior vice president, Jeremy, was dysfunctional, and nobody was talking about it. There was not enough trust at the company to make this invisible challenge visible.

The company was reaching a crisis point: It was no longer profitable, customers were growing increasingly unsatisfied, and daily operations were chaotic. Fred sensed that a breakthrough, high-performance team was needed because the company was going downhill fast.

For some months, Fred had been in denial, hoping it would all work out. Then came the shouting matches with Jeremy, who would commit to Fred, peers, and customers to do things and then just would not do them. When confronted, Jeremy offered a host of excuses. "I did not think that is what you meant," he would say.

This dysfunction went on for three years.

Then I facilitated a meeting in which the team communicated to Jeremy why he was a detrimental presence. The team sought to understand where Jeremy was coming from (he said they couldn't function without him). They asked clarifying questions. They took turns speaking and listened fully. The conclusion: no one could trust Jeremy to do what he said he was going to do. But Jeremy did not see he needed to change. Jeremy, who was really good at self-preservation, started to lobby other executives to support him.

In meetings with the leadership team, it became more and more apparent to everyone that Jeremy was the problem. Because of this, the leadership team was not able to create the foundation of trust necessary for a breakthrough, high-performance team. Fred was afraid to terminate Jeremy, reasoning that a poor senior vice president was better than no senior vice president. Despite the fear of changing the status quo, Fred let Jeremy go. Jeremy was shocked and insisted the company could not survive without him.

A funny thing happened, however. The leadership team without Jeremy became instantly functional. Trust was quickly established, and now the path was clear to establish a breakthrough, high-performance team.

The remaining four leaders were now able to make changes to better serve clients, to make more money, and to improve efficiencies. Fred had almost lost the company, but turned it around once the invisible was made visible and dealt with in a proper manner. Fred learned his lesson: you cannot afford to enable one person to create an environment that turns everyone dysfunctional. Like the old adage, one bad apple can spoil the whole barrel.

Quit Flipping Others' Threat Switches

To build trust, we need to quit flipping on the amygdala Threat Switches of other team members.

Allow me to explain. A great technique for building trust, previously mentioned, is to ask clarification questions. Let's take a deeper dive into that topic.

Companies don't hire people, they hire brains. And to get the collective benefit of the brains, meetings of brains are called.

Conflicts happen during a meeting when a brain feels it hasn't been heard. So, in a business meeting, the unheard brain repeats itself over and over. "What I said was awesome; clearly they didn't hear, so I will repeat myself," is what the brain is thinking.

When you ask a clarifying question or paraphrase what you heard, other brains say, "That proves you are listening." Not being heard triggers the brain's Threat Switch, the good old amygdala.

The amygdala doesn't trust anybody or anything. When you think of the amygdala, you should think *fear.* The amygdala Threat Switch controls the way we react to certain stimuli (like negative comments in a meeting) that our brain sees as potentially threatening.

I see brains come together and flip each other's Threat Switch all the time.

Here is something I have had to say more than once at a meeting I have facilitated: "You just spent forty-five minutes talking about trust, and you said respect is important, but you just spent fifteen minutes interrupting each other."

Old habits are hard to break. We also switch on other people's amygdala when we use words such as, "I think you are wrong," "I disagree," and, "How did you come up with that?"

Sometimes, I personally trigger The Threat Switch when I say, "I don't think you get it." Immediately I can see it in the eyes. Some people get very mad, which ironically proves my point.

Using Axioms to Build Your Personal Trust Brand

When we talk about the concept of business and/or behavioral tools in my workshops, one of the most impactful is a list of personal behavioral axioms. These axioms are the rules that you want to abide by, in terms of self-regulation and dealing with others.

Behavioral axioms fall under the concept of emotional intelligence. Let me praise the work of Daniel Goleman, who for twelve years wrote for *The New York Times*, reporting on the brain and behavioral sciences. According to Goleman, in his 1995 book *Emotional Intelligence*, the five elements of emotional intelligence are self-awareness, self-management, self-motivation, empathy, and influence.

One of the ways to enhance emotional intelligence is to utilize behavioral tools. These axioms can act as guidelines for your behavior, covering self-management in the context of emotional intelligence—which flows into self-awareness and self-motivation.

The goal is to focus on my life's purpose: to care, encourage, and inspire. What type of behavior do I have to engage in to assist me in remaining on-purpose? To help me stay on-purpose, here are the five behavioral axioms I've abided by for the last twenty years:

▶ **AXIOM 1.** *Do not allow fear to drive thoughts or actions.*

In my experience with people, most are triggered very quickly and very easily in terms of shifting into fear. When you are in a state of fear, you can only engage in three actions: fight, flee, or freeze. Fear represents survival, and people slip into survival mode all the time. Unfortunately, when the brain perceives some type of threat, it immediately goes into a survival state, which triggers a fear-driven reaction. I want to make sure that's not where I am coming from. When I feel myself triggered, I tell my brain to *knock it off! We are not going to die.* I turn the amygdala (lizard brain) off.

▶ **AXIOM 2.** *Seek first to understand.*

I realized in my business career, most people don't really invest much in understanding the purposes, concerns, and circumstances of other people. We naturally tend to focus on what we believe, what we think, and what we want. It's imperative for me to always position myself to seek first to understand where the other person is coming from. Before I express anything in terms of what I want, or what I need, I want to first focus on their purposes, concerns, and circumstances. That's the only way I have found that allows other people to focus on my purposes, concerns, and circumstances. First, you must care before you are cared for.

▶ AXIOM 3. *Things happen; I don't know if they are good or bad until hindsight.*

We posture about things a lot and make all sorts of assumptions. We have beliefs about other people's intentions and go on about how terrible something that happened is. In truth, many times, in hindsight, it's not that bad at all. The classic example is when people lose their jobs, the initial reaction is to think that it is horrible. It's a threat, so they go into a state of fear. They wonder how they are going to survive and pay the bills. But when you talk to them six months later, they've typically found a new job, and they are far happier than they were before. So, what happened wasn't such a bad thing after all. The reason I think this is important: it allows me not to get too vested in my positioning, either way, as things happen in my life. It allows me to not get too depressed or excited either way. I know to wait and see what events lead to. It's a mechanism that helps regulate my behavior.

▶ AXIOM 4. *In life, it's 10 percent what happens and 90 percent how I deal with it.*

I have found this axiom to be true. If people don't really think this through, however, many will reverse the percentages, placing a lot of blame and frustration about what other people do and the things that happen to them. The truth is, stuff happens. It happens to all of us. The key is not to get too caught up in that and position yourself as a victim. It's up to you to decide how to deal with it—which puts you in a much stronger position of power.

▶ AXIOM 5. *Every positive, carried to the extreme, becomes a negative.*

The very things that allow us to be successful in business and to have enriching relationships can be carried to an extreme, becoming negatives. Personality characteristics carried to an extreme often become negatives. If you're a high-dominant personality, that is positive in terms of leadership. You are a person who doesn't mind taking charge, you have clarity, and you're about getting things done. On the other hand, if these characteristics go to the extreme, you can become a tyrant. Another classic behavioral position is a high level of influence. These folks can persuade and motivate others, which is a powerful skill. But if it is carried to the extreme, these people can often end up being viewed as shallow and feckless.

A Closing Thought

What do you stand for? For me, having a set of personal axioms has helped guide me to breakthrough, high-performance team success. Axioms are the rules that you want to abide by, both in terms of self-regulation and in dealing with others.

AXIOMS FOR HIGH PERFORMANCE

Build Trust

- Do not allow fear to drive your thoughts or actions.

- Seek first to understand.

- Things happen, and you don't usually know if they are good or bad until hindsight.

- In life, it is 10 percent what happens to you and 90 percent how you deal with it.

- Every positive, carried to the extreme, becomes a negative.

CHAPTER 4

Master Conflict

Breakthrough, high-performance teams learn how to master conflict.

This is a cautionary tale about Sheila, a trusted executive with significant tenure at her company, who was not able to master conflict. (Plot spoilers: cautionary tales do not have happy endings.)

Sheila knew the strategic initiative project she led was a mess; however, she did not know what to do about it. Essentially, Brent and Larry, two experienced team members with grand ideas and hearty professional ambition, had hijacked the initiative. Worse yet, their actions had begun to put the project at risk.

"Something has to change, or the project is doomed," Sheila thought to herself. Many in the team felt alienated by Brent and Larry. Team members said their behavior left them feeling like observers more than participants, second-class citizens more than contributors, and afterthoughts more than teammates. "I vow to do whatever it takes to save the project," Sheila told herself.

Upon reflection, Sheila realized the offending duo had been selected initially for their project management experience and get-it-done attitude. In hindsight, however, Sheila later discovered there was one key ingredient missed in team selection. That ingredient is a trait crucial to high-performing teams: empathy. Moreover, this oversight was particularly embarrassing given its status as one of the company's core values and the management team's recent training in emotional intelligence.

How could this oversight have happened? With the backing of the company's CEO, whom I had known personally and professionally for more than ten years, I was brought in to lead a multiday instruction on breakthrough, high-performance teams with all of the company's managers and executives.

Some of the lessons did not come easy to the management team. The training started with an exercise to help each person understand behavioral drives. Conflict, for example, generates different responses in different people.

"When faced with conflict, there is a natural tendency to drop into a state of fear: fight, flight, freeze, or appease," I explained. "This is a biological response triggered by the amygdala in the brain."

"So, you are saying we need to avoid conflict?" asked Sheila.

"No, quite the opposite," I explained. "You need to master conflict. Identifying and understanding how fear works and our response to it is the first step towards having *command* over this natural response."

There were other struggles. Empathy as a concept is relatively easy to grasp; however, to practice empathy consistently and model it for others is another matter completely.

The phrase which resonated most loudly with the management team to describe this scenario was "below the line/above the line" behavior. Being *below the line* described the state in which a manager was acting in accordance with his or her fear, emotionally and not rationally. Decision-making in this state was suboptimal and manifested itself in various ways: meetings tended to be more argumentative, discussions veered toward determining *who* was right versus *what* was right, or managers either opted to withdraw or take actions to cover their own rears. This type of behavior was poison to a business that wanted to thrive and grow.

Identifying and naming this conduct allowed managers to operate with a common language for regulating behavior. It was a tool for gently challenging one another—holding one another accountable for pulling themselves up from operating below the line. Not only had the training provided increased self-awareness, but it also led to better self-management. Managers moved from making decisions in a state of fear to making them rationally, thoughtfully and mindfully.

Sadly, it was too late for Sheila and the strategic initiative team. The CEO had to step in and fix the problem by removing one of the offenders and having Sheila step aside as the project's champion. Eventually, the strategic initiative succeeded, and Sheila went on to champion other projects. Overall, the experience served as a valuable lesson in training exercises for staff and future managers on mastering conflict.

Mastering Fierce, Yet Positive Conflict

In today's extremely rapidly changing dynamic business environment, CEOs recognize that the right kind of fierce conflict is essential to stay on top of ongoing challenges and issues within their organizations. The tension behind the right kind of conflict is not personal attacks or cynicism. The right kind of fierce conflict is centered on the tension between what is right for the business and right for the customer.

Such tension centers around this dynamic imperative: how can the company do what it does faster, cheaper, better, and still make a profit? Because if the company is not focused on this ever-evolving conflict, then customers will leave the company for competitors who are faster, cheaper, and better.

Fierce yet positive conflict is supported by following agreed-upon breakthrough, high-performance team behavior norms. Here are the steps.

- **Step one.** Engage in curiosity-driven discussion.

- **Step two.** Demand that everyone expresses his or her opinion.

- **Step three.** Rather than criticize others' ideas, build on others' ideas.

- **Step four.** Make the invisible visible by naming the elephants in the room.

- **Step five.** Ask clarifying questions.

- **Step six.** Restate what you heard.

Because of competitive pressures, breakthrough, high-performance teams are constantly identifying and attacking roadblocks and bottlenecks that prevent the company from continuously improving strategies and tactics, allowing the company to honor the dynamic imperative of faster, cheaper, and better. The process of attacking roadblocks and bottlenecks requires a fierce, positive, customer-directed culture of creative conflict.

Training to Master Fierce Conflict

One of the keys to creating a breakthrough, high-performance team is to train the team on mastering fierce conflict. Many teams that I train think beforehand that I will want them to avoid conflict in the workplace. Actually, that is a horrible idea. Fierce conflict is necessary to create breakthroughs.

Here is an exercise for developing a unique definition of fierce conflict for breakthrough, high-performance teams in your company. The process begins with some structured conversations around these topics:

- What does fierce conflict look like in our team?

- How do we build fierce conflict?

- What will prevent us from succeeding?

- What is our current state when it comes to fierce conflict?

- What is the desired state we want when it comes to fierce conflict?

- What behaviors are above the line?

- What behaviors are below the line?

This exercise is designed to get these issues out in the open. To master fierce conflict requires a frank, open discussion of what is currently going on and what you want for the future.

Axioms for High Performance

Master Conflict

- Master the skill of fierce conflict.

- Engage in curiosity-driven discussion.

- Demand that everyone expresses his or her opinion.

- Rather than criticize others' ideas, build on others' ideas.

- Make the invisible visible by naming the elephants in the room.

- Ask clarifying questions.

- Restate what you heard.

Chapter 5

Achieve Commitment

A chieving true team commitment is more difficult than it appears.

Edward, a hardworking leader who was well respected by his team, was the CEO of a company with annual revenues of $30 million. Edward could see the company tripling in revenues, if only they could solve a nagging problem.

Surveys confirmed that the company's customers were becoming increasingly less satisfied. After years of growth, satisfaction scores were starting to fall.

I was brought in by Edward to help identify the issues. He wanted to know what would have the greatest impact on raising customer satisfaction levels from less satisfied to very satisfied. One issue that was quickly identified was a lack of training for the company's new hires.

Edward and his team decided it was important to increase the amount of training given to the young, enthusiastic college graduates the company was hiring. There was nothing wrong with this pool of new hires; they just needed more direction and mentoring.

Saying you need to do something and then achieving it are two different things. With the help of a flip chart, I worked with Edward and his team for thirty minutes to carefully sculpt the exact wording of what they wanted for the training. Why did this take a half-hour? Wording was debated, and that was healthy, because none of the team was shrugging off the assignment and being lazy.

That's what achieving team commitment requires. With that commitment, the company did not just pay lip service to their new training program. Achieving real commitment to training resulted in a dramatic rise in satisfaction scores. And as a result, Edward was pleased to see revenues climb from $30 million to $100 million in four years.

Why is Achieving Commitment Hard?

To achieve commitment, here is what you don't want: meeting discussion loops going around in circles and silent members just looking at their watches and playing with machines while the vocal duke it out.

Let me repeat for emphasis: Saying you need to do something and achieving the commitment to actually do it are two different things.

Here are a few of the reasons why:

- **Never assume.** After a subject has been discussed, the team leader/members should never assume there is agreement on the issue and end the meeting. Almost always, there is no agreement.

- **Nodding is not agreeing.** When the leader asks (or states) that there is agreement on an issue, team members might acquiesce via slight up-and-down head nods. That doesn't really mean agreement.

- **Don't mistake silence for consent.** Sometimes, few members contribute to the discussion, and many of the silent members don't agree with the conclusion.

- **Talking is not agreeing.** Maybe the discussion goes on endlessly, with participants repeating their opinions because they're afraid they were not heard the first time. The meeting ends without any conclusion.

As a result of the above, two decades of experience have taught me the members have not bought into the decision or conclusion.

You know there has not been true commitment when: participants leave the meeting and give extraordinarily different versions of the meetings conclusions and decisions; participants tell their team, "I disagreed, but this is what was decided;" participants are surprised and shocked by the decision's implementation; and participants do not take ownership of the decision.

What Commitment Really Means

Not achieving commitment is a huge problem in business. I constantly hear from clients that they can no longer trust that people in their business will do what they have committed to do. Examples are:

- People do not show up for meetings
- People cancel agreed-upon meetings with little or no notice
- People are constantly late for meetings
- People do not meet their agreed-upon completion date for tasks
- People do not keep their promises

Such behavior seems to have become acceptable in many organizations. You often hear, when people do not meet their commitments, the following: "No problem." This is not a good way to respond to people who do not meet their commitments. It makes this behavior somehow OK, and if you are going to have a highly successful company, this behavior is not OK.

In my work concerning becoming a high-performance team, one of the common behavior axioms the team members abide by is, "When I commit, it's do or die." As a result, team members are focused on making sure everyone understands and takes ownership of the commitments they have made, and commitments are not made haphazardly.

One key to making sure everyone understands and agrees to a team decision is to write the decision on a flip chart or overhead screen. It is amazing how often the decision is changed or adjusted by putting it in writing where everyone can see it.

Don't Accept Meetings on Auto-Pilot

In building high-performance teams, we teach the importance of setting ground rules for meetings. Meetings should have start and stop times, stay on track, and not be allowed to go down rabbit holes. That means having an agenda and staying on course.

Sharon Rich, author of *Your Hidden Game: Ten Invisible Agreements That Can Make or Break Your Business*, shares this story about a real-life example of how meetings can go awry.

"Many years ago, I was working for a large charitable nonprofit. Every week I attended a meeting with twenty-two other people to brief Richard, their extremely hands-off senior vice president. These meetings were very frustrating. Their only purpose was to update Richard. There was no coordination, no decision-making, and no valid benefit for any of us sitting through everyone else's reports.

"And yet we did, week after week after week.

"To make matters worse, Richard was consistently late. When he wandered in twenty to thirty minutes late, he would waste even more time, taking several minutes to connect and share personal chit-chat with a few of his closest associates in the room.

"Once the meetings began, they generally took three to four hours. They went on so long, people would be called out of the room to other meetings. When it was an absent person's turn to report, we would all have to wait while someone went to find them.

"When the meetings finally dispersed, spin-off complaint sessions took place in the bathrooms, the kitchen, and behind closed doors in private offices, where people blew off steam about the waste of their time—which wasted an additional thirty to sixty minutes of the workday.

"This was no soft agreement. I did the math. I added up everyone's salaries and hourly rates and discovered we were wasting nearly $500,000 every year in this one recurring meeting. That was a lot for a nonprofit that had to raise every penny of that money.

"In my world, if you see it, you have to say it. So, in the most nonthreatening way possible, I asked Richard, 'This meeting is costing the agency half a million dollars a year, and I'm wondering, does this make sense? Isn't there a more efficient way to brief you?'

"Of course, it wasn't that Richard wanted to waste everyone's time. He had just never really considered it. The meeting hadn't started as a gathering of twenty-two people. It had simply grown to that size and scope over time. It wasn't anyone's intention, yet no one had thought to question it, and the meeting had become another costly example of 'just the way we do things here.'" (Rich 2018)

Personal Brand: Accountability

Pop quiz: Who is the person you first think of when asked who can you most depend on to meet his or her commitments?

The person I always think of is John Tidgewell. John has been a teammate of mine for over seventeen years, and everyone who deals with him knows he will do what he commits to doing. You don't need to worry about following up with John or reminding him of his commitment. John is so well known for his consistent adherence to meeting commitments that it is a significant element of John's personal brand.

If you want to be well thought of by your peers and team members, make it a point to always meet your commitments. In today's environment, that is a competitive advantage. The same can be said for breakthrough, high-performance teams. One of the guiding principles of a breakthrough, high-performance team is to meet personal and team commitments. Think of it as a do-or-die attitude.

Every breakthrough, high-performance team should develop its own definition of peer accountability.

How to Achieve Commitment

When it comes to building high-performance teams, I am not a theorist. I am a pragmatist. In twenty years, I have trained thousands and thousands on the methods of building high-performance teams, and no one has ever said it doesn't work. On the contrary, I have countless testimonials on its power. People write: "This has changed my life." That is brain candy for me.

So, in practical terms, here is how to start. Assemble your team and get them to answer these four questions:

- What does achieving commitment look like in our team?

- How do we build it?

- What will prevent us from succeeding?

- How do we go from the current state to the desired state?

Achieving commitment means making sure everyone has their opinions heard. As the leader, you need to seek clarity. You want people fully committed to the team discussion, with no one undermining the team decision. This is not a democracy. Sometimes the leader wants team input; the leader is tasked with making the ultimate decision based on factual and emotional input from the team.

Clarity Is Crucial

For clarity, communication must be in writing. Where we are, where we need to go, and what steps we may need along the way: it needs to be written down. As the old Hollywood joke goes, verbal agreements aren't worth the paper they are written on. Using a flip chart or whiteboard is a great idea.

When making decisions, write them down, and then ask the group, "Is this what we have agreed upon?" To get commitment and buy-in from the group everyone must commit to the decision.

Communications should promptly cascade through the organization. Team members are accountable to drill down the decisions. They should share decisions with their direct reports within twenty-four hours, either verbally by phone, or preferably in person. Email alone does not cut it. A conversation allows for questions and/or suggestions and helps control rumors. New or transferring employees can cause rumors or go against the group's decision if they are not properly informed. Be sure to update your team as you receive new information.

When explaining decisions, team members should avoid using defensive words that show a lack of commitment, such as "I disagree," or "if it were up to me." Instead, try to use piggyback words like, "and I would like to add to your topic."

Here is the worst thing that can be said: "I disagree, but here is what the group decided." That is a sure way to undermine commitment.

When objectives aren't met by team members, ask clarifying questions: Why? Are there personal issues or lack of resources? Hold people accountable for their actions or commitment to the group or project.

Be sure to put goals in writing. Set dates and times for benchmarks and next meetings, then use these as a timeline for completion.

Achieving commitment is about getting the team to believe in what they are doing, and to have that permeate the culture of the business. I have faith in the saying: "Beliefs drive culture. Culture drives behavior. Behavior drives results."

When I Commit, It Is Do or Die

I added this axiom to my tool kit about ten years ago. What I've realized is that in the current culture, it's common for us to commit to things we don't do. In business, that plays out in things like committee meetings, where people agree to do something, but they don't really own it. If something else comes up, a person can be quick to shift priorities.

The challenge with that approach is, whether we know it consciously or subconsciously, we begin to distrust that person. Failure to meet commitments can create a trust issue within a team. I think a huge part of trust is for team members to be comfortable that they have each other's back. It's important that when team members make a commitment, each person can depend on the others to do what they said they were going to do. You are a much more powerful, more respected and valuable team member when people recognize you as someone who does what you say you will do. What a relief it is not to have to constantly follow up on what has been committed to.

To avoid creating this trust issue, we need to be far more careful about what we commit to. The idea is, when I commit, I will be very careful what I commit to, because once I do, I am going to make it happen. It is a great self-management tool, because it does put you in a position of committing where you want to and need to, and not committing just to appease someone else at the moment.

Axioms for High Performance

Achieve Commitment

- When I commit, it is do or die.

- Team members focus on what we are deciding, and as a result, team members take ownership of the commitment.

- Be careful to what you commit to; do not make commitments lightly or haphazardly.

- Understanding you will own the decision enhances the quality of the discussions.

- Because brains are inherently lazy, they like to conserve energy; when brains know that the matter is truly important, they go into high gear.

- A key element of commitment is the thematic goal; we all have different agendas, but we can all agree on a thematic goal.

CHAPTER 6
Enhance Accountability

A s a young man, I remember several enjoyable discussions with Joe, my hardworking father-in-law, regarding a variety of topics. Quickly I realized how much importance Joe placed on what his peers at the chemical plant thought about things.

In fact, Joe was more affected by his peers' ideas, beliefs, and opinions than he was by his bosses' or even most of his family members'. Joe also told me stories about how important it was to him to not let his fellow workers down at work. Joe clearly cared far more about what his peers thought of him than his boss.

I have experienced this power of peer accountability for more than twenty years as a facilitator of Vistage CEO groups. One might think these CEOs, most of them owners of their own companies, would not be swayed by what others think. Surely these entrepreneurs must be rugged individualists.

In my decades of experience, however, these CEOs are highly motivated to make sure they don't let their fellow CEO group members down by not meeting their commitments to the group.

Here is an example. After a meeting in which the Vistage group had processed an issue for one of the members, this member (let's call her Marilyn) committed to renegotiating a buyout deal with her partners. Two months later at a group meeting, Marilyn reported to her fellow CEOs that she had met with her advisors, developed an alternative buyout proposal, met with her partners, and they had recently signed a new deal. Just before the meeting, Marilyn confided to me that it was one of the most difficult things, both emotionally and from a business standpoint, that she has ever done. But Marilyn knew it was the right thing to do and was determined to meet her commitment to the group.

Because of those conversations with my father-in-law, Joe, and my business experiences with the power of peer accountability with CEOs like Marilyn, I encourage breakthrough, high-performance teams to leverage peer group accountability rather than to focus on traditional reporting structure accountability.

I learned at an early age the power behind the concept of peer pressure and the related concept of peer accountability. Breakthrough, high-performance teams learn to be skilled at leveraging peer accountability.

Developing Peer Accountability

A breakthrough, high-performance team should create a definition of accountability to each other. Here are the steps the team should take to define where the team stands when it comes to peer accountability:

1. **Determine what accountability looks like for the team.** Here are questions to discuss: What does accountability look like when you are taking the lead? Do we commit to follow through, whether results are good or bad? Do we agree to maintain great communication with each other, our other team members, and our customers?

   Not completing projects can become an epidemic, and that doesn't build trust. What do you say when a team member does not complete a project? Often people will say "no problem" to be cordial. However, saying "No problem" when goals or deadlines are not met is a problem. Every team member should be concerned about building his or her own personal brand. The brand to strive for is one that people trust.

2. **Agree on how to build accountability.** Do not use excuses for not completing tasks or making deadlines. Do what you said you would do, and do it on time. Set goals, put it down in writing, and hold yourself and teammates accountable. Make the invisible visible

when roadblocks appear. Ask questions like, "Do we need to allocate more resources?"

As a leader, lead by example through coaching or mentoring your team members. Pay proper attention to communications with existing employees, new employees, or members at other stores. Understand change is part of the process. Embrace change or something new, especially new technology. Breakthrough, high-performance teams embrace new technologies.

3. **Determine what would prevent accountability.** Be careful about what you commit to, and do not overcommit. Be cautious when saying no to a commitment. Instead, try to work out alternate solutions or options. Maximize other resources within your grasp from other stores or departments. Keep the customer's viewpoint in mind, looking at things the way a customer would view the situation.

When it comes to accountability, ask, "How do we go from current to desired outcomes?"

Strong individual accountability leads to better team accountability. Delegate more tasks as employees become more competent. Allow for alternative ideas with the same end results in mind. Here is what to strive for: More and better communication at all levels (from top on down) and consistent customer experience at all stores, locations, or divisions.

Axioms for High Performance

Enhance Accountability

- My personal brand includes accountability.

- We are obligated to accept responsibility and disclose results in a transparent manner.

- We determine what accountability looks like for the team.

- We agree on how to build accountability.

- We determine what could prevent accountability, so we head it off.

CHAPTER 7

Focus on Results

Jay Thiessens, the hardworking founder and CEO of B & J Machine and Tool in Sparks, Nevada, joined my Vistage CEO peer group in 1997. He seemed like any other harried business owner, and the other CEOs respected his insights.

None of us knew the painful secret Jay was hiding. Jay's threat switch was on. Fear had held him back for years.

"I don't have time to read this," Jay would often say of contracts and paperwork. At night at home, his loyal wife Bonnie would help him sort through the paperwork at the kitchen table or even in bed.

None of the managers at his company, none of his peer CEOs at Vistage, and certainly not I, knew that Jay could not read.

"You're better at legalese than me," Jay would tell his general manager and hand him legal documents like contracts. For seven years, that general manager had no clue he was the only one reading the documents.

At the age of fifty-six, Jay made the brave decision to come clean to our Vistage group. I had met with him because I knew something was not right. Jay might disappear for a week at a time. Later, I learned he was so depressed he could not leave his bedroom.

Through the years, Jay had learned to compensate by being a great listener. He rarely forgot details and had a solid grasp of math, especially geometry.

Jay had been reluctant to join my group because he thought he wouldn't measure up to his college-educated peers. I knew he was a high school graduate, and he was very successful in business. So, I assumed he could read. Six months later Jay shared his secret with me.

Jay was initially extremely reluctant to tell the other twelve CEOs and business owners in the group, because he felt the members would at best think less of him or at worst belittle him behind his back. After being in the group for more than a year, he confessed his shameful secret in one of the group's monthly meetings.

To Jay's shock and surprise, the group members immediately expressed their respect and awe at what Jay had accomplished in business and life without the ability to read. One member suggested that Jay meet with an adult reading coach he knew.

Jay did meet with the reading coach, and over the course of three years, became an adept reader. To this day, Jay works with the State of Nevada, helping with the state's literacy program, and has been recognized nationally for his work in literacy.

Jay was one of six national winners of the National Blue Chip Enterprise Initiative Award, sponsored by the U.S. Chamber of Commerce and MassMutual. The award recognizes small businesses that have triumphed over adversity.

Jay credits his spectacular rise—from having a terrible personal secret to helping thousands with literacy challenges— to allowing himself to be vulnerable to his Vistage Chair and Vistage team.

I believe the real secret to Jay's success was when he decided to switch off The Threat Switch and focus on the result.

"There is no shame in not knowing how to read," said his wife, Bonnie. "The shame is not doing anything about it."

Getting Results

What does focusing on results look like for high-performing teams?

Breakthrough, high-performance teams create a team goal and set a timeline for its completion. To understand the goal fully, the team seeks clarity by asking questions, taking notes, and holding follow-up meetings to track progress, check for understanding, and check on assigned tasks.

Sharing information is critical too. These teams cascade communications of the project's status to all affected. They stay on top of it by sharing updates or issues in a timely fashion. These teams utilize the twenty-four-hour goal of communicating status updates to all members. The intent is to prevent rumors from generating and/or confusion. Breakthrough, high-performance teams take charge of communications; they do not default to the grapevine or water cooler gossip.

Making the Transition

Becoming a breakthrough, high-performance team is a process. Remember those before-and-after ads on TV? The situation in the *before* part of the commercial is bad, but by using the advertiser's product, everything becomes much better. The same concept is true with breakthrough, high-performance teams. Consider these transition steps.

From	To
Focused on "my" team	Focused on "peer" team
Inside-the-silo perspective	Out-of-silo perspective
Communicating activities	Communicating ideas
Single-perspective problem-solving	Multi-perspective problem-solving
Group of coworkers	High-performance teammates
Scoring points for me	Helping the team win

In the before world, the silo perspective dominates. A silo mentality can be a typical attitude in many organizations. This occurs when departments or groups do not want to share information or knowledge with other individuals in the organization. Leaders tend to be more concerned with protecting their teams. At staff meetings, they tend to just report on the activities they are engaged in. Their view of others is that they are all just coworkers competing with one another.

Maybe that is your *before* picture.

Now, what can an organization transition to with a breakthrough, high-performance team approach? Time and again I have taken part in amazing transformations.

The *after* picture can be a dramatic shift to a focus on a peer team. These teams realize that a silo mentality reduces efficiency of the overall operation, reduces morale, and contributes to a lack of productive results.

A breakthrough, high-performance team realizes that everyone is in this together. The ideal is to have everyone working together so the team wins. That takes readily communicating ideas, getting multiple perspectives to solve problems, and seeing each other as high-performance teammates.

There is a good share of not letting others flip your threat switch, too. Breakthrough, high-performance teams know when someone is flipping their Threat Switch, and that they have the power to switch it off.

Dos and Don'ts to Get Results

What should be done consistently to get results? Here is a brief list:

- Do keep the project alive by staying engaged.

- Do put goals or milestones in writing.

- Do bring goal-related issues into group meetings for processing and clarification.

- Do measure success or current progress by setting timelines.

- Do make it visual by keeping score.

- Do have accountability for team members.

What are the don'ts that will prevent you from succeeding? Here are a few:

- Don't overload people with too much to do on a daily basis.

- Don't have a lack of constant communication.

- Don't fail to meet goals or timelines.

- Don't fail to prioritize projects currently in progress.

- Don't omit a list of expectations to complete goals on time.

From Here to Eternity

It is possible to transform from an organization that has spotty execution of projects to the desired state of full-on execution of completed projects. More importantly, the more the organization does so, the better it gets at it. Breakthrough, high-performance teamwork is not an event; it is a process. The real winners are the organizations that create this approach as part of their culture. That will produce results now and into the future.

Axioms for High Performance

Focus on Results

- We focus on results over activity.

- We avoid the silo mentality.

- We rely on a peer team approach.

- We communicate ideas with the team.

- We solve problems using a multi-perspective approach.

- Together, we win as a team.

PART III

BRAINPOWER GAME CHANGERS

Chapter 8

Execution Teams and Strategic Teams

A brainpower game-changer for your organization is to understand the difference between execution teams and strategy teams. Every business has execution teams because that is how things get done. But not every business has strategic teams to make sure things are getting done *right*.

Let's compare and contrast execution teams and strategic teams when it comes to creating breakthrough, high-performance teams.

Execution Teams Get Things Done

Execution teams typically work within their silos of responsibility and are all about getting things done. I often hear complaints from leaders and managers about the lack of success in such teams in meeting their goals and objectives.

The following graphic is a depiction of some typical execution teams and is far from exhaustive. I have placed names at the tops of the silos to indicate some team leaders.

Examples of Execution Teams

Pat	Ben	Bobbi	Juan	Raj	Maria
IT	Marketing	Sales	Service	Operations	Finance
Coworkers	Coworkers	Coworkers	Coworkers	Coworkers	Coworkers

My experience is most people work their buns off in execution teams. The problem is the execution teams keep running into roadblocks and bottlenecks that slow them down or even prevent them from doing their jobs.

Contrast That to Strategic Teams

Strategic teams want to know what is getting in the way of high performance.

Strategic teams focus on identifying execution team roadblocks and bottlenecks and attacking them. Strategic teams are drawn from people from the execution team silos. When issues are processed, you want to have a cross-section of representatives from the execution teams.

Two axioms to remember: We are better together, and sharing ideas creates clarity. The following graphic is a depiction of a strategic team. The team members are pulled from the execution teams.

Example of a Strategic Team

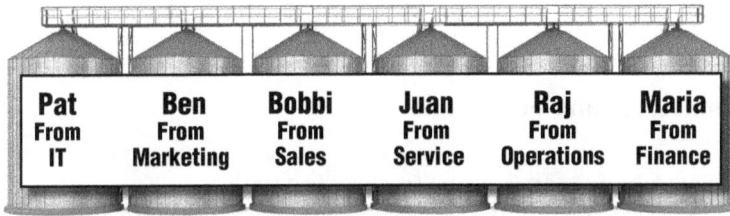

Pat	Ben	Bobbi	Juan	Raj	Maria
From IT	From Marketing	From Sales	From Service	From Operations	From Finance

Strategic teams look at the whole process, seeking out obstacles that get in the way of efficient, effective, and high-quality execution, and as the bug company says, "Stomps them dead!"

Strategic teams are constantly asking:

- What's getting in our way?

- What's negatively impacting our quality?

- What do we do about it?

In my work, when the strategic teams work together, there is a moment of realization, like in cartoons when a lightbulb goes on above a character's head. In this *aha* moment of insight, the strategic team realizes that most of the organization's problems are internally caused. Instead of asking the execution teams to be more effective and efficient, the strategic team discovers it has the power to change things for the better. This is when high-performance breakthroughs happen.

Let me repeat this for emphasis: in my years of experience, *most of the roadblocks and bottlenecks are internally caused.*

This is both the bad news and the good news. This is good news because strategic teams have the complete ability to identify and eliminate or dramatically reduce internal roadblocks and bottlenecks.

The strategic team's job is to clear the path.

Axioms for High Performance

Execution Teams and Strategic Teams

- We need execution teams and strategic teams for breakthrough high performance.

- We have execution teams to get things done.

- We have strategic teams to find the roadblocks and bottlenecks that hinder execution.

- Strategic teams ask, "What's getting in our way?"

- Strategic teams ask, "What's negatively impacting our quality?"

- Strategic teams find out what needs to be done to allow execution teams to be more effective and efficient.

CHAPTER 9

Training the Team to Facilitate Issue Processing Meetings

I n the 1992 movie *A League of Their Own*, Tom Hanks' character, Jimmy Dugan, talks about baseball being hard. "It's supposed to be hard," says Dugan. "If it wasn't hard, everyone would do it. The hard is what makes it great."

During the course of facilitating CEO meetings over the past twenty years, I have learned that facilitation is hard. A skillful facilitator has a hard job: understanding and explaining the difference between being responsible for process versus content and who is responsible for what.

The group is responsible for content, and the facilitator is responsible for process. Content is what is to be discussed, and process is the way the discussion will play out.

Facilitation requires the ability and willingness to:

- Be in command of the process
- Not slip into content
- Monitor and keep time requirements
- Ensure everyone has the opportunity to participate
- Maintain order
- Make sure the process steps are not violated

There is one more thing a facilitator needs to be willing to do.

Ask the Provocative Questions

The facilitator will often think of provocative questions when a team is having a discussion to process an issue. The questions might be, "What are the consequences of that," or, "If you couldn't do that, what would you do?" It is the facilitator's duty to ask such provocative questions.

A provocative question serves to provoke the team. Such questions can reenergize a conversation that is losing steam. The result is more team energy and creativity. Facilitators must know it is their job to challenge the group.

In my experience, provocative questions result in the team coming up with action items they would not have come up with had the conversation not been reenergized. Provocative questions can take the team to out-of-the box thinking and get the creative juices flowing. To do this takes vulnerability on the part of the facilitator, because the facilitator risks asking an inappropriate question.

But it is vitally important for facilitators to follow their natural wonder and curiosity. The benefits of asking the risky questions far outweigh the safety of not asking a question that should be asked.

Four Types of Business Meetings

There are four primary types of business team meetings. The meeting type needs to be decided at the outset to avoid confusion, enhance efficiency, and hold a successful meeting. The facilitator needs to know which one of the four meeting types is needed:

- **Report- and information-oriented.** This is the most time-consuming meeting in terms of preparation. Strong facilitation is important, because these meetings can easily devolve into tedious meetings filled with extraneous input. If more than one person will be presenting, decide time increments for individual presentations and hold presenters accountable. Add spice to the meeting via energetic introductions of each speaker, smooth transitions that carry the theme throughout the meeting, and a comprehensive conclusion. What you say and how you say it can create a well-constructed meeting.

- **Decision-making and problem-solving:** These are the most complicated meetings. The facilitator must determine who gets the floor, how long the meeting lasts, who speaks, and how long individuals take the floor. You should conduct process checks and summaries of progress during the meeting. Be aggressive about not letting people get off track. Keep the discussion on topic and hold attendees to agreed-upon behavioral axioms for the meeting. This is a "results" meeting; therefore, keep things moving along and encourage the attendees to make a decision or solve the problem.

- **Creative and brainstorming.** These meetings are less focused on process and require a more relaxed facilitation approach. The most important job of the facilitator here is to ensure that all participants get an opportunity to express their thoughts, and that individuals do not talk over each other. It is also important to create a nonjudgmental atmosphere where ideas are openly expressed without right/ wrong comments. As with all meetings, be sure to document decisions.

- **Training and skill-building.** These meetings require extra preparation for the facilitator. The role is a combination of teaching and facilitating. Also, be sure to provide sufficient time for the attendees to really get involved in the training/skill-building process, and schedule time for the members of your class to reinforce what they are learning. Your attendees will learn by participating, not only by listening. The more they are involved, the more questions they ask, the better the results will be.

Meeting Process Axioms

An axiom is a statement that everyone believes is true, such as "supply equals demand" or "the only constant is change." To make meeting process run smoothly, participants should agree to the following axioms:

- Prepare for the meeting.
- Arrive and start on time.
- Share all relevant information.
- Raise hands when you want to speak.
- Create and manage time increments.
- Record outcomes.
- Record action items.

Meeting Behavioral Axioms

In addition to process axioms, there are also behavioral axioms that all participants agree to hold to as the truth:

- Stay mentally and physically present.

- Contribute to meeting goals.

- Let everyone participate.

- Listen with an open mind.

- Think before speaking.

- Avoid repetition.

- Stay on point and on time.

- Attack the problem, not the person.

How to Identify Meeting Issues

Facilitating the handling of an issue begins with some thoughtful work. A big part of the breakthrough, high-performance team process is to create an issue statement for a concern or opportunity to be processed.

Don't attempt to take on everything at once. Start by handling one issue at a time. Here are the steps to cover in creating an issue statement to guide the team:

- **Step one.** Begin by stating the goal as clearly as possible.

- **Step two.** If the issue remains unresolved, define the impact on your people, products, and services. List any other things that may be affected by this unresolved issue.

- **Step three.** Next, consider what happens if the issue is resolved. What would the impact be on people, products, and services?

- **Step four.** Then consider the estimated monetary Impact. What would be the impact in dollars and cents when the issue is successfully resolved?

- **Step five.** Now on to background information: What are the facts? Answer the questions around the issue of what, why, how, where, who, and when.

- **Step six.** Now describe what has been done or tried so far. Typically, an issue has not been totally ignored. What have you done and what have you considered doing?

- **Step seven.** Then ask for the help you need from the breakthrough, high-performance team. What are the possible solutions, alternatives, and possible consequences?

- **Step eight.** Before concluding, there are some final questions to consider. What are the takeaways? What are the next steps? What are the action items? What is the update schedule (when does the presenter want to give an update on the issue)?

How Does This Work in Real Life?

Every organization is different, and yet many issues are consistently found in many of the organizations I have worked with. In the following table, the left column contains typical issues. This is not an exhaustive list; it is kept short so it is manageable. In the right column is a corresponding list of what needs to be determined for the organization to handle the issue.

Create a chart like this:

Issues/Concerns/Opportunities	Purpose and How-Tos
1 Our costs are higher than our competitors'	1 How to become the low-cost producer
2 Our inventory records and organization are a mess	2 How to create an organized inventory management system
3 Our customer service is inconsistent and slow	3 How to computerize all customer service functions

To provide three more sets of examples, the following are concerns that could be discussed in a meeting and the resulting purpose/how-tos the team would want to determine:

Concern: Many customers are buying our competitor's products on their computers

Purpose: How to generate 50 percent sales via the Internet in three years

Concern: It takes forty-five days to process a home loan

Purpose: How to process a home loan in fifteen minutes

Concern: We are slow to respond to changes in the marketplace

Purpose: How to change company culture to be entrepreneurial

After you have determined the concern or opportunity to attack, next hold a meeting to address the issue. With proper preparation, handling this issue should take just an hour. The following section explains how to do just that.

Create a How2 Issue Statement

A next step is to plan the meeting by using a tool called the How2 Issue Statement. Here is a template to use.

HOW2 ISSUE STATEMENT

HOW2...

State the goal as clearly as possible

If unresolved...

Impact on people, products, services, etc.

If resolved...

Impact on people, products, services, etc.

Estimated monetary impact...

Impact in dollars when successfully resolved

Background information...

What, Why, How, Where, Who, When

Done so far...

What I have considered/done so far

Help I need from my breakthrough, high-performance team...

Possible solutions, alternatives, possible consequences

Where to find more info

Critique of current plan

Issues Worksheet with Time Increments

Done correctly, it should only take sixty minutes to process an issue. The intent should be to get everyone involved and to stick to the allotted time segments There is nothing to be gained for letting debates drag on. Think of this like a game of Beat the Clock. The team needs to win—and win within the allotted amount of time.

TIME	AGENDA
10 min.	**Present topic or issue** Review the HOW2 issue sheets emailed to team before the scheduled meeting.
15 min.	**Clarification questions from group**
15 min.	**Solutions/recommendations from group** What are the team's options or solutions? Identify if solution is an individual or team issue, and how it may affect the team.
5 min.	**What did the group hear?** What are you being held accountable to solve? Set time limit to resolve or respond back to group (e.g., 15/30/60 days)
5 min.	**Write down action items** This leads to personal/team accountability. If compressed for time, this can be done with a follow-up group email within one week's time by the presenter.
5 min.	**What is the impact of issue? (social, economic, employee, customer)** Always put a dollar value on each issue using best judgment. Be consistent.
5 min.	**Clarify the issue processing results for group and test for understanding** Including accountability for action items and set time frames.
60 min	**Total time of meeting**

Make it a high priority for all team members to participate while sticking to the agenda and time limits. Otherwise, the process limits the group's capacity to perform and accomplish tasks together. Remember to keep the eye on the clock. The task needs to be finished in sixty minutes.

One More Thing: Are There Any Process Questions?

Make it part of the process to improve the process. I recommend using a checklist approach for the postmortem analysis. Here is a handy checklist of questions to help you improve your breakthrough, high-performance team approach.

- ✔ What went well with the process of solving the issue?

- ✔ What could have been improved about the process?

- ✔ What should we stop doing as a team?

- ✔ What should we continue doing as a team?

- ✔ What should we start doing as a team?

- ✔ Where are we in the process?

- ✔ Have all team members followed through with their commitments?

Lastly, use a timer and stay on track to honor the process. Honoring and valuing people's time is a matter of respect.

Axioms for High Performance

Training the Team to Facilitate Issue Processing Meetings

- Tackle issues with an issue statement.

- Processing an issue can be done in sixty minutes.

- For every issue, develop a "How2" statement.

- Part of the process is improving the process.

CHAPTER 10

Creating a Breakthrough, High-Performance Team Culture

L et me conclude by praising the work of Patrick Lencioni, author of *The Five Dysfunctions of a Team*.

In his book, Lencioni offers an instructive leadership fable. Here's the plot summary (but no spoilers): Kathryn Petersen, Decision Tech's CEO, faces a leadership crisis: Uniting a team in such disarray that it threatens to bring down the entire company.

Will she succeed? Will she be fired? Will the company fail? Barnes & Noble calls it a powerful yet deceptively simple message for all those who strive to be exceptional team leaders. Lencioni's tale serves as a reminder that leadership requires as much courage as it does insight.

Like Lencioni, my life's passion is to help those who are striving to be exceptional team leaders.

Ah, but here's the rub when it comes to teams. In interviewing hundreds of team members in dozens of companies, I have found a common theme: most team members consider themselves to be coworkers rather than team members.

The question becomes, how do we evolve from a coworker relationship to a breakthrough, high-performance team relationship? The answer to that is the essence of creating a breakthrough, high-performance team culture.

First, let's recap how to create breakthrough, high-performance teams.

Creating Breakthrough, High-Performance Teams (BHPT): The Summary

For those of you who like the *Reader's Digest* or *Cliff's Notes* version, here is the quick summation of what we have learned and how to apply it:

- **The Threat Switch: Enemy Number One of Breakthrough Teams.** There is a part of our brain that is designed for one thing: survival. This brain part often dictates our behavior, consciously and subconsciously. In neurosciences, it is called the amygdala, and it is often referred to as our lizard (reptilian) brain. This part of the brain helps us survive by dictating we choose fight, flight, or freeze. I call this lizard brain The Threat Switch. This ancient part of our brain is only the size of an almond (amygdala is Greek for almond), but it has huge power. When the amygdala detects a possible threat to our survival, it immediately hijacks the brain and engages our fight, flee, or freeze reaction mechanism. This is quite a natural action.

- **Put Aside What Comes Naturally.** Fear is natural. The Threat Switch is natural. Breakthrough, high-performance teams put aside what is natural. I have spent the majority of my life deliberately studying human behavior, taking the praxeology approach, which is the deliberate study of human behavior from a streetwise, practical approach. This practical approach is the converse of theory. Praxeology has taught me there are five steps to create breakthrough, high-performance teams (BHPT).

- **BHPT Step One: Build Trust.** In the beginning, there must be trust. In fact, trust is foundational for creating a breakthrough, high-performance team. If a high level of trust cannot be created, then the team will never progress into a breakthrough, high-performance team. Genuine vulnerability (that state of mind that allows for curiosity and learning) is crucial to developing trust. Interestingly, most people perceive vulnerability in themselves as a weakness. Ironically, these same people perceive another person's willingness to be vulnerable as a strength.

Certain ground rules have to be agreed upon to allow team members the safety to be vulnerable in meetings when you are creating breakthrough, high-performance teams.

- **BHPT Step Two: Master Conflict.** In today's extremely rapidly changing, dynamic business environment, business CEOs recognize that the right kind of fierce conflict is essential to stay on top of ongoing challenges and issues within their organizations. The tension behind the right kind of conflict is not personal attacks or cynicism. The right kind of fierce conflict is centered on the tension between what is right for the business and right for the customer. The tension centers around this dynamic imperative: how can the company do what it does faster, cheaper, and better, and still make a profit? Because if the company is not focused on this ever-evolving conflict, then customers will leave the company for competitors who are faster, cheaper, and better.

- **BHPT Step Three: Achieve Commitment.** Not achieving commitment is a huge problem in business. I constantly hear from clients that they can no longer trust that people in their business will do what they have committed to do. Examples are people who do not show up for meetings, people who cancel agreed-upon meetings with little or no notice, people who do not meet their agreed-upon completion date for tasks, and people do not keep their promises. This seems to have become acceptable behavior in many organizations. You often hear "No problem" when people do not meet their commitments. This is not a good way to respond to people who do not meet their commitments. It makes this behavior somehow OK, and if you are going to have a highly successful company, this behavior is not OK. Breakthrough, high-performance teams abide by the axiom, "When I commit, it's do or die."

- **BHPT Step Four: Enhance Accountability.** A breakthrough, high-performance team should create a definition of accountability to each other. Here are three ways to define where the team stands when it comes to peer accountability: *1. Determine what accountability looks like for the team.* Here are questions to discuss: What does accountability look like when you are taking the lead? Do we commit to follow through, whether results are good or bad? Do we agree to maintain great communication with each other, our other team members, and our customers? *2. Agree on how to build accountability.* Do not use excuses for not completing tasks or meeting deadlines. Do what you said you would do, and do it on time. Set goals, put it down in writing, and hold people accountable.

Make the invisible visible when roadblocks appear. Ask questions like, "Do we need to allocate more resources?" *3. Determine what would prevent accountability.* Be careful about what you commit to, and do not overcommit. Be cautious when saying no to a commitment. Instead, try to work out alternate solutions or options. Maximize other resources from other stores or departments. Keep the customer's viewpoint in mind, looking at things the way a customer would view the situation.

- **BHPT Step Five: Focus on Results.** Breakthrough, high-performance teams create a team goal and set a timeline for its completion. To understand the goal fully, the team seeks clarity by asking questions, taking notes, and holding follow-up meetings to track progress, check for understanding, and check on assigned tasks. Sharing information is critical, too. These teams cascade communications of the project's status to all affected. They stay on top of it by sharing updates or issues in a timely fashion. These teams utilize the twenty-four-hour-goal of communicating status updates to all members. The intent is to prevent rumors from generating confusion to and/or from team members. Breakthrough, high-performance teams take charge of communications; they do not default to the grapevine or water-cooler gossip.

- **Properly Deploy Execution Teams and Strategic Teams.** Execution teams typically work within their silos of responsibility and are all about getting things done. I often hear complaints from leaders and managers about the lack of success in such teams in meeting their goals and objectives. Strategic teams focus on identifying execution team roadblocks and bottlenecks and attacking them. Strategic teams look at the whole process, seeking out obstacles that get in the way of efficient, effective, high-quality execution.

- **Train the Team to Facilitate Issue-Processing Meetings.** Meetings are a way of business life. There are four types of meetings: report and information oriented, decision-making and problem-solving, creative and brainstorming, and training and skill-building. The facilitator and the group have key roles. The group is responsible for content, and the facilitator is responsible for process. Content is what is to be discussed, and process is the way the discussion will play out. Meeting facilitation requires the ability and willingness to be in command of the process, monitor and keep time requirements, ensure everyone has the opportunity to participate, maintain order, and make sure the process steps are not violated.

What Comes Next: Cultural Guiding Principles

"Talent wins games, but teamwork and intelligence win championships," said Michael Jordan. According to the *NBA Encyclopedia*, Jordan, formerly of the Chicago Bulls, is the greatest basketball star of all time. Jordan played on six NBA championship winning teams. Do you think the Chicago Bulls players saw themselves as coworkers or team members?

The NFL trophy for the Super Bowl is named for Vince Lombardi, the coach who led the Green Bay Packers to five championships. It was Lombardi who said, "Individual commitment to a group effort—that is what makes a team work, a company work, a society work, a civilization work." Do you think those Green Bay Packers saw themselves as coworkers or team members?

The "we're just coworkers" belief has a devastating impact on team performance, in that most people do not perceive their team as a resource when dealing with challenges and opportunities. They are far more likely to approach an issue by going it alone than leveraging the wisdom and support of their team.

There is a way to make sure that wisdom and support are leveraged. Management guru Peter Drucker famously said that "Culture eats strategy for breakfast." What Drucker was saying is strategy can't succeed without the support of the people. Therefore, it is imperative to create a culture that is about sustaining your breakthrough, high-performance team.

In the world of sports, the Chicago Bulls and the Green Bay Packers had a winning culture. Those cultures were not built overnight (and they did not last forever). So, how can you sustain high-performance teams?

Mine Success Stories Around Your Core Values

Every business has core values, although some have not formally stated what they are. Basically, core values are the guiding principles that drive an organization's conduct, both internally with employees and externally with customers. Here are a few examples of core values from Vistage member companies:

- Go the extra mile for customers.

- Do whatever it takes to get the job done.

- We value integrity, which means doing what you say you will do.

- Quality is job number one.

The list of possibilities is mighty long. Core values are a decision that company leaders make. To create a breakthrough, high-performance culture, I recommend you adopt these core values:

- We are better together.

- Sharing ideas creates clarity.

- Commitment defines and evidences character.

- The team is greater than the individuals.

- If your Threat Switch gets flipped, you have the power to turn it off.

Now, as you create breakthrough, high-performance teams, gather success stories of these core values in action. To get you started, I have included several examples throughout this book. As you mine your stories, I would enjoy hearing from you. Please share these stories with me so they can inspire others through my writings, trainings, and teaching.

I wish you the best as you not only create breakthrough, high-performance teams, but also as you create a breakthrough, high-performance team culture.

AXIOMS FOR HIGH PERFORMANCE

Creating a Breakthrough, High-Performance Team Culture

- Understand The Threat Switch is the enemy of breakthrough teams.

- Put aside what comes naturally, which is freeze, fight, or flight.

- The goal is to build high-performance teams.

- BHPT Step one: Build Trust.

- BHPT Step two: Master Conflict.

- BHPT Step three: Achieve Commitment.

- BHPT Step four: Enhance Accountability.

- BHPT Step five: Focus on Results.

- Properly deploy strategic teams to clear the way for execution teams.

- Train the team to facilitate issue-processing meetings.

- Mine stories to sustain a breakthrough, high-performance team culture.

APPENDIX

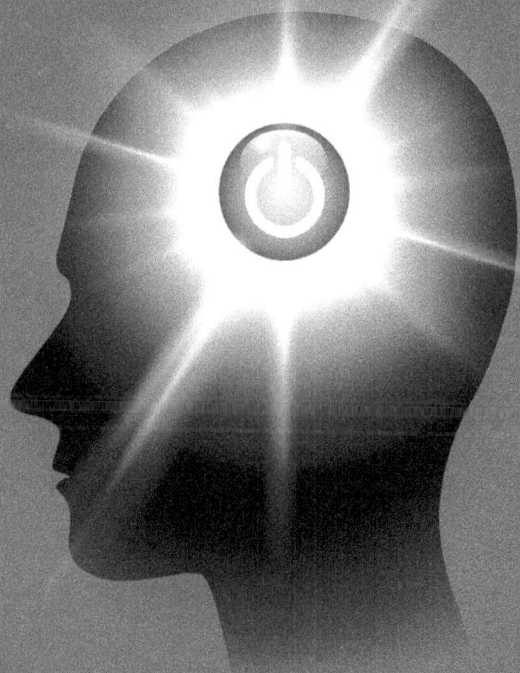

Acknowledgments

M y thanks and deep appreciation to the following individuals who helped make this book possible.

My wife, Geralyn, whose unwavering support, counsel, and encouragement have saved me from myself more times than I can possibly count.

John Johnson, my Vistage Chair and lifelong friend, who taught me the importance of seeking clarity in all that I do.

Ken Monroe, President of Holt of California, whose participation and assistance in developing the Breakthrough, High-Performing Team concept was crucial to the development of this book.

A special thanks to John Tidgewell and Michael Frampton for investing the time in reading, critiquing, and offering suggestions to improve this book.

And to my clients and members over the past twenty years who have given me the honor of being their peer, coach, and friend. The stories in this book are straight from these relationships.

WORKS REFERENCED

Goleman, Daniel. *Emotional Intelligence*. London: Bloomsbury Publishing, 2014.

Hubbard, Jan. *The Official NBA Encyclopedia*. New York: Doubleday, 2000.

Lencioni, Patrick. *The Five Dysfunctions of a Team: Team Assessment*. San Francisco: Pfeiffer, 2007.

Rich, Sharon. *Your Hidden Game: Ten Invisible Agreements That Can Make or Break Your Business*. Oceanside, CA: Indie Books International, 2017.

About the Author

Randy Yost sees himself as a lifelong student and teacher of the study of human behavior.

Two seminal life/business events served as the foundation of his decades of study of applied human psychology: first, a botched surgery as a young man that threatened his ability to walk, and second, a career as a bank turnaround CEO. Both experiences caused Randy to delve deeply into why individuals and teams behave the way they do.

In over forty years in business as a bank CEO and CEO coach, there is only one business truth that never changed for Randy: For the majority of businesses, the only sustainable competitive advantage is their people. After all, it is the only element of companies that's truly unique and cannot be duplicated.

Since 1996 Randy has been a group chairman for Vistage Worldwide Inc., an international organization of CEO peer advisory groups, and is a principal of Business Mastery Consultants, a Sacramento-based executive coaching and team development firm. Randy has served as coach and confidante to hundreds of CEOs, business owners, and senior executives.

Prior to his Vistage chairmanship, Randy served as president, CEO and chairman of the board for community banks and bank holding companies in Oregon, Nevada, and California.

To inquire about booking Randy as a speaker or for bulk orders of this book, contact him at randy@bizmasters.biz.

www.ingramcontent.com/pod-product-compliance
Lightning Source LLC
Chambersburg PA
CBHW031951190326
41519CB00007B/762